An orange-painted pavilion at Compton Acres, Poole, Dorset, in a Japanese garden created in 1914 by T. W. Simpson. The orange-red colour was thought erroneously to be thoroughly Japanese.

Japanese Gardens in Britain

Amanda Herries

A Shire book

Published in 2001 by Shire Publications Ltd,
Cromwell House, Church Street, Princes Risborough,
Buckinghamshire HP27 9AA, UK.
(Website: www.shirebooks.co.uk)

Copyright © 2001 by Amanda Herries.
First published 2001.
Shire Album 387. ISBN 0 7478 0500 8.
Amanda Herries is hereby identified as the author of this
work in accordance with Section 77 of the Copyright,
Designs and Patents Act 1988.

British Library Cataloguing in Publication Data:
Herries, Amanda
Japanese gardens in Britain. – (A Shire book)
1. Gardens – Japan
2. Gardens – Japan – Design
I. Title
712'.0952
ISBN 0 7478 0500 8

Cover: *The Japanese garden at Tatton Park, Cheshire, constructed in 1910 for Alan de Tatton.*

ACKNOWLEDGEMENTS
For permission to reproduce photographs, thanks are due to Jennifer Campbell, daughter
of Ian Campbell, page 35 (both); Heale House, Wiltshire, page 30 (left); Patricia Layhe,
page 23 (both); the National Monuments Record (Crown Copyright), pages 4, 27, 30 (bottom); the National Trust at Tatton Park, page 22 (bottom); and Takashi Sawano, pages 17
(left), 24, 37 (top and middle). Special thanks to the staff of the Royal Horticultural Society
for their help and to the Society for permission to photograph and use images from the
Lindley Library: pages 8 (bottom left), 10 (bottom), 13 (bottom), 15 (all), 16 (all), 17 (bottom
right), 18, 20 (all), 21 (all), 25 (bottom, both), 26 (all), 31 (both), 32 (all), 33 (all), 34 (all). The
front cover photograph is by Clive Nichols. All other photographs are by the author.

Printed in Malta by Gutenberg Press Limited, Gudja Road,
Tarxien PLA 19, Malta.

Contents

Part of the garden at Katsura Imperial Villa near Kyoto, Japan. Completed in 1658, it is a perfect example of the landscaped stroll garden.

Introduction

'A garden in Japan is a representation of the scenery of the country.' So wrote Josiah Conder in his book *Landscape Gardening in Japan* in 1893, the single greatest influence on Japanese garden design in the West. To the average reader of that book, Japanese gardening meant *bonsai* trees, or trees and shrubs pruned into unnatural shapes, and gardens adorned with 'oriental' ornaments. Western gardeners imitated what they saw, though frequently with little understanding of the principles required to create the authentic effect. It is said that when a senior Japanese diplomat visited the Japanese garden created by Sir Frank Crisp, at Friar Park near Henley-on-Thames in Oxfordshire, in the early years of the twentieth century, he exclaimed, 'How beautiful – we have nothing like this in Japan!' The diplomat was undoubtedly complimenting Crisp, unaware of any sense of irony. Whether Crisp was pleased with the comment is not known, but his version of a Japanese garden was just an approximation of the garden it was imitating.

Japanese gardens, their design and plants have intrigued and stimulated the West since the Portuguese and Spanish first

A general view of the Japanese garden, created *c*.1906, at Friar Park, Henley-on-Thames, Oxfordshire, as it was when the gardens were open to the public. Frank Crisp wrote a very anecdotal guide to his gardens and was immensely proud of them.

A private garden near London, devoted to the Japanese ideal, created in 1905 and enhanced in the 1920s. Lanterns, bridges, summer houses and a villa were shipped from Japan to complete the effect.

visited Japan in the mid sixteenth century. Weather conditions and soils were known to be compatible, so the discovery of unknown trees and shrubs led to great excitement. The gardens, however, were much more difficult to interpret in a Western culture. The many Japanese gardens created in Europe and America at the beginning of the twentieth century, when the passion for the newly discovered Japanese arts and culture was at its height, were usually Western interpretations of Japanese ideals. At best they were a distillation of Eastern influence within a Western framework, and at worst they simply displayed a Japanese 'touch'.

In Japan the garden had evolved over

Tatton Park, near Knutsford, Cheshire. A typical example of the English Edwardian interpretation of a Japanese garden, with a modest tea house nestling in a terraced landscape.

5

Ginkaku-ji, the Silver Pavilion in Kyoto, Japan, originally built in 1485. The raked sand garden and mound appeared later. The purpose of the mound is unknown but it has been given various interpretations. The garden has become one of Kyoto's most celebrated images.

some twelve hundred years, with several distinct and separate styles emerging over the centuries. Buddhism had a profound influence on Japanese garden style, but a garden aesthetic was developing long before Zen Buddhism introduced the dry landscape garden so frequently (but incorrectly) thought to be the essence of a Japanese garden. Religion, both the native Shinto and the introduced Buddhism, played a major role in garden design, and it was often an ignorance of the significance of these basic elements which made the Western interpretations look different from their Eastern inspirations. Cultural differences also had an effect: the West failed to appreciate the asymmetry essential to Japanese garden design, or the importance of creating a balance between the *in* and the *yo* (from the Chinese *ying* and *yang*, the two opposing elements from which everything is composed). Nowhere is this more apparent than in the typical English garden, so often overcrowded and overgrown. Yet it was the English who were so particularly fascinated by the beauty, tranquillity and order of the Japanese garden.

This tea-house garden, in the grounds of the Shugaku-in Imperial Villa outside Kyoto, is famous for the strikingly modern-looking 'sleeve-shaped' lantern. The complex dates back to the seventeenth century.

6

The stroll garden at Sento Gosho (retired Emperor's Palace) built in 1630 and designed by the Emperor. Offering ever changing panoramas, it is one of the most peaceful gardens in Kyoto.

Sources of inspiration

Many of the fundamental ideas of the Japanese garden were brought initially from Korea and China by itinerant priests and other travellers whose knowledge and skills proved influential in all areas of Japanese artistic life. Gardens are described as early as the seventh and eighth centuries, and these were already influenced by Chinese geomantic rules, governing the location of a garden and the inclusion of its chief components: water, rocks, plants and ornaments.

Stroll and viewing gardens

During the Heian period in Japan (794–1185) Imperial palaces and the residences of noblemen were built with large gardens, which always included a lake with islands, bridges and park-like scenery. Some of these still survive and now form the basis of public parks. The most famous treatise on gardening in Japan, still consulted universally today, was probably written in the eleventh century by a courtier and poet, Tachibana no Toshitsuna. The *Sakuteiki* (or *Essay on Garden-making*) covers general principles and offers information on all aspects of garden-making, focusing on the importance of stone in a garden. It also includes historical anecdotes and taboos. Much of the information is in accord with Japanese gardens built over the centuries and is still relevant to garden designs throughout the world today. The gardens of the Heian period developed into what are nowadays described as stroll gardens and viewing gardens.

Dry gardens

This garden style emerged over centuries of turbulent warfare interspersed with periods of peace. Zen Buddhism, introduced to

7

At Katsura Imperial Villa a pavilion looks out on to a miniature view of Amano Hashidate, a bay on the coast of the Sea of Japan, one of Japan's three most famous views. The scaled-down representation is typical of many garden views.

The garden at Nijo Castle in Kyoto was built for the visit of the Emperor in 1626 by a famous garden designer. A shallow shore-line and beach are suggested by the smooth, carefully selected pebbles by the lake.

(Above left) In 1893 Josiah Conder published *Landscape Gardening in Japan*, in which he described gardens in great detail with many illustrations. It had a great influence on Western builders of Japanese gardens. The 'Large Lake Garden' would have been a typical stroll garden.

(Above right) An early Japanese postcard view of a lake garden in Tokyo, c.1890.

Japan from China during the Kamakura period (1185–1333), emphasised 'being in harmony with the cosmos . . . achieving a oneness with nature . . .' It appealed to a people who already venerated nature through their own indigenous beliefs, known as Shinto, or 'the way of the gods'. Shinto had been influenced by

'Water takes its shape from the container into which it flows, with both good and bad results. Therefore you should always exercise the greatest care with the design of your ponds.' This advice from the *Sakuteiki* is still fundamental to the use of water in a Japanese garden.

The *karesansui* garden at Kofuku-ji in Kyoto might be interpreted as islands in a turbulent sea. The gravel is raked at least once a day.

Buddhism, introduced from China in the sixth century, and over many generations Shinto and Buddhism have developed a complementary relationship which still exists today. Zen Buddhism introduced a new element: the practice of seeking enlightenment through meditation. Followers could strive to achieve this goal through concentrated self-awareness when engaged in even the most mundane activities. This is why some of the finest gardens in Japan are attached to the great temples in Kyoto, where monks used the acts of creating and tending the gardens, as well as the contemplation of the results of their labours, as part of the meditation process. Many of the most famous of these gardens consist of raked gravel, or gravel and rocks, without any living plants. These are known as 'dry gardens', or *karesansui*. It was also Zen monks who first recorded their appreciation, over a thousand years ago, of the mosses that grew in many of the temple gardens in the dappled light coming through the maple trees.

The Abbot's Garden at Ryoan-ji is considered the supreme example of an abstract Zen garden. Its origins are mysterious, its creator and age unknown. Probably dating from the late fifteenth century, it was 'discovered' in the 1930s and swiftly became world-famous.

(Right) The grounds of Saiho-ji are like an enchanted forest, carpeted with more than one hundred varieties of moss. Designed originally in 1339 by the monk Soseki Muso, who considered gardens as an aid to meditation, the mosses only began to grow some three hundred years later.

Tea gardens

The last significant garden style also emerged from Japan's troubled past and was created in connection with what in the West we call the tea ceremony, perfected in the late sixteenth century. *Chanoyu* (literally meaning 'hot water for tea') is indeed a ceremony, although not a formal one. A host invites guests to share the enjoyment of the refined, powdered green tea and to appreciate the prized artefacts with which it is prepared. The *chanoyu* takes place in apparently simple surroundings that have been carefully designed to reinforce the idea of a richness in the soul complemented by a natural but restrained setting. A tea house is normally very plain, almost rustic, and

Josiah Conder's illustration of a tea garden and its enclosure.

Tea house and garden in the grounds of the Eikan-do temple in Kyoto. Stepping stones are a key feature, leading towards the tea house, first passing the water basin. The symbolic washing of hands and mouth is an important stage in the 'way of tea'.

usually small and totally unfurnished apart from a single flower arrangement and scroll with calligraphy to focus the participants' thoughts on the ceremony. It always stands in a small garden: the guests are transported from the turbulence of everyday life into the tranquillity of the world of tea as they pass through the confined space. The 'tea garden', or *roji*, is deliberately enclosed – an important aspect of many Japanese gardens – by a perimeter fence, frequently of bamboo. It always contains one or more lanterns to light the way, stepping stones glistening with sprinkled water as a silent gesture of welcome, and a stone basin to hold the water for the ritual cleansing of the hands and mouth before entering the tea house. There may be shrubs and trees, but the hard-packed earth around them and around the stones is always swept clean, perhaps leaving one or two fallen leaves at the appropriate season. The whole effect appears natural but is carefully contrived to give a reproduction of nature, a larger space, in a small area.

The view from the Bosen-tei room at Koho-an temple is a representation of a nearby famous beauty spot. It is designed specifically to be viewed from a kneeling position within the room and is enhanced by the framing given by the *shoji* (paper screens) and the panelled walls of the tea house.

11

(Above left) Rocks at Ryugin-an, part of the Tofuku-ji temple complex in Kyoto. 'Always begin by positioning a particularly well-shaped stone and let it dictate the arrangement of all the other stones' (advice given in the *Sakuteiki*).

(Above right) The powerful, thrusting rocks at Daisen-in, in the grounds of Daitoku-ji, Kyoto, form one of Japan's most famous gardens, created in the fourteenth or fifteenth century. This is a three-dimensional rendition of a Chinese black ink (*sumi*) landscape painting.

Another feature of Japanese gardens is the use made of *shakkei*, meaning 'borrowed scenery'. A garden design will always take note of the background behind and above the garden, so that this can become a part of the garden without seeming incongruous in any way. Usually this is achieved so successfully that the visitor to the garden is not even aware of accepting the background as part of the view.

A Japanese garden will also include many elements commonly found in Western gardens but employed in a different way. Stones and rocks are the most important and significant of these and will be found in almost every Japanese garden as a deliberate part of the design. Water plays a part in most gardens, be it a lake, waterfall, stream or pond. Sometimes the water is merely suggested, by a stream created by carefully selected flat stones or gravel raked to represent a pond, lake or ocean with water breaking around rock islands. Bridges, fences, gates and ornaments, particularly lanterns but also water basins and bamboo water

Part of the garden at Ginkaku-ji, the Silver Pavilion, in Kyoto. The lushly planted pond garden is a surprising contrast to the more famous abstract garden a few feet away.

pipes, are also common features.

The plants used in a Japanese garden are selected specifically to contribute to the overall design. The main effect is of the greenness of the planting, with a seasonal splash of colour provided by blossom or perhaps the exotic flowering of a wisteria or peonies – and frequently the astonishing block of solid colour produced by tightly pruned azaleas. Trees are often carefully trained to contribute to the design, which is always governed by a deliberate asymmetry and the maintenance of a balance between the opposing elements of *in* and *yo* that are crucial to the success of the design.

A private garden in Yokohama in the 1930s, with a number of unusually large lanterns. Private gardens of this size are rare in Japan today.

13

Early explorers

Japanese plants arrived in the West as a by-product of commercial and religious expeditions rather than as a result of gradual exploration and discovery. The Spanish and Portuguese first went to Japan purely in search of financial gain and at a time when missionary zeal was at its height. Their commercial activities soon led to competition from the English, Dutch, Russians and other European powers. The Dutch East India Company emerged as the most important, responsible for exporting the majority of the goods reaching the West by the seventeenth century. Thousands of pieces of porcelain, as well as lacquer wares, paper folding screens and other items, all of which frequently had representations of Japanese flowers, trees and gardens, gave the fascinated West a glimpse of unfamilar treasures.

However, in 1639 Japan finally tired of the proselytising efforts of the Portuguese, and all foreigners were expelled. Foreign trade was severely restricted: minimal contact continued with China and the only western activity was with the Dutch East India Company, confined to an outpost near Nagasaki, with staff serving one-year terms of duty. Japan remained in its self-imposed isolation for over two hundred years until an American, Commodore Matthew Perry, forced trading and consular relations in 1854. This was swiftly followed by treaties with Britain, Russia and Holland.

(Above) A large Imari 'charger' showing women admiring *bonsai*, prunus and pine in a fenced garden; late seventeenth or early eighteenth century. Huge amounts of Japanese porcelain were exported to Europe during the seventeenth and eighteenth centuries, despite Japan's isolation. They helped to give a glimpse of Japanese scenery to the intrigued West.

(Right) Folding screen showing seasonal flowers and trees; eighteenth century. Painted in ink and colours on gold paper, such screens were used in Japan as room dividers and were sometimes exported to Europe, where they found their way into private art collections.

Cover of a rare book of wood-block print pictures of irises, possibly produced by the Yokohama Nursery Company at the beginning of the twentieth century. Named for Engelbert Kaempfer, the iris in all its stunning shades became immensely popular in England.

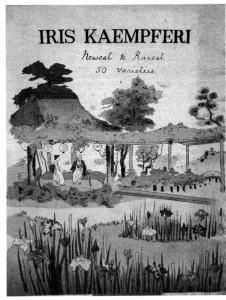

IRIS KAEMPFERI

Newest & Rarest
50 varieties.

Engelbert Kaempfer, a German doing his year of duty as physician with the Dutch East India Company in 1690, was the first foreigner to send information on plants to the West. Many trees and shrubs now familiar in Western gardens were first described in his *Amoenitates Exoticae*, published in 1712. Skimmia, aucuba, hydrangea, magnolia, prunus, tree peonies, ginkgo, camellias and many others were painted in painstakingly accurate watercolours, accompanied by descriptions of their history, and their medical and economic use. In 1728 Sir Hans Sloane arranged to have Kaempfer's *History of Japan* translated into English – this provided the first written insight into some of the mysteries of that far-off land.

Carl Pehr Thunberg, a Swede also working as a medical officer, managed to travel between Nagasaki and Tokyo (then called Yedo) in 1775, gathering about a thousand species of

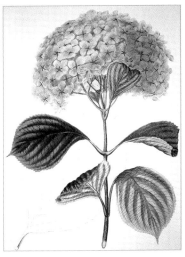

(Above) One of the many delicately coloured irises depicted in the Yokohama Nursery Company's book. The book contains over thirty different examples, ranging from white to deep purple and vibrant pink.

(Right) *Hydrangea otaksa*, a plate from the *Flora Japonica* published in 1835 by von Siebold and dedicated to Kaempfer and Thunberg.

Prunus japonica (above left) and *Prunus mume* (above right), from von Siebold's *Flora Japonica*.

plants, including a great many lilies, and describing them and his travels in great detail. Thunberg was particularly inventive in his efforts to obtain and hide his specimens. His *Flora Japonica*, a cornerstone for Japanese taxonomic botany, was published in 1784.

Philipp Franz von Siebold, a German eye doctor also on secondment with the Dutch East India Company in 1823, studied garden design and the local flora in his off-duty hours. He was the first to bring back actual plants to the West and shipped 458 specimens to Holland in 1830. When he retired he lived outside Leiden in a rustic house with gardens he named Nippon, the Japanese name for Japan, from where he continued to mastermind the shipment of Japanese plants to Europe, despite the difficulties in obtaining the plants and the effect on them of the rigours of the sea journey. He opened a

Wisteria chinensis, or Chinese wisteria, from von Siebold's *Flora Japonica*, published in 1835. Its stem twists anti-clockwise, whereas *Wisteria floribunda*, a native of Japan, twists clockwise. The flowering racemes on the Japanese wisteria are far longer than those on the Chinese, and the effect when trained on a pergola is stunning.

An early Japanese photograph of the annual 'viewing' of a wisteria arbour, c.1890. Even today the seasonal blooming of wisterias, irises, azaleas, and in particular cherry blossom, as well as the autumn colours of maples, draws huge crowds of admirers.

nursery where he grew trees, chrysanthemums, lilies, peonies and many other shrubs. Over 30,000 specimens, together with drawings by Japanese artists, were on view at the Japanese Herbarium in Leiden by 1843 and were reported on for the first time in England by Professor Zuccarini in the *Gardener's Chronicle and Agricultural Gazette* in April of that year.

Von Siebold's contribution to the introduction of Japanese plants to Europe cannot be overemphasised, coming as it did a decade or so before Japan reluctantly opened her ports. When that happened, in 1854, there was a mad rush from both Europe and America to see at first hand its curiosities. Three Americans – S. Wells Williams, James Morrow and Dr George Rogers Hall – were collecting in the early years, as was Carl Johann Maximowicz, a Russian who became friends with von Siebold and returned to St Petersburg with a significant haul of specimens, seeds and living plants.

The Englishman John Gould Veitch (1839–70), a member of the famous nursery family from Chelsea in London, first travelled in Japan for a year in 1860. Veitch brought back the curious 'umbrella pine' (*Sciadopitys verticillata*), white and black pines

(Below) *Lilium auratum*, an illustration from the *Lilies of Japan* catalogue produced by the Yokohama Nursery Company in 1907.

(Above left) Clipped and trained *Pinus thunbergii* in Japan. These pines may be well over one hundred years old and are clipped at least twice a year.

17

James Herbert Veitch (1868–1907) was stunned by the sight of lilies growing in great quantities in the wild in Japan. This is his photograph of *Lilium auratum* growing at Kew Gardens for his book *Hortus Veitchii* published in 1906.

(*Pinus pentaphylla* and *Pinus thunbergii*), Japanese larch (*Larix kaempferi*) and many others, including the golden ray lily (*Lilium auratum*), which helped to start the huge fashion for lilies in the West that has been fully exploited over the years by the Japanese. Charles Maries, who worked for Veitch, also brought back the first live specimens of *Magnolia stellata*. Veitch acquired new premises for his nursery activities on the southwestern outskirts of London in Kingston-upon-Thames, at Coombe Wood, and stocked the new land with his Japanese plants. In due course this was made into water gardens and might fairly be said to be the first Japanese garden in Great Britain.

Veitch wrote at length about his travels, as did his fellow plant-hunter, the equally famous Robert Fortune (1813–80). Fortune had travelled extensively in China and arrived in Japan in 1860. He explored for two years, sending specimens and plants home, including several bamboos and *Aucuba japonica*, and making acute observations about his journeys. The gardening magazines of the day make mention of the sales of plants following the travels of both Veitch and Fortune. Veitch's plants, sold in October 1863, made between £400 and £500 at auction for 295 lots (equivalent to about £6000 to £8000 in 2000). Fortune's, in the same month, included amongst the 628 lots one hundred that were between 2 and 3 feet high (60–90 cm). The difficulties of gathering and packing the plants are well described by Fortune, and it is remarkable that so many survived the long sea journey (at least four months) in the airless, dark and cramped cases.

The 1870s were marred by stormy internal politics in Japan, when few foreigners were encouraged to continue their journeys of discovery. But the door had been opened, and the West was full of enthusiasm for the newly discovered '*Japonisme*': exhibitions of Japanese art opened all over Europe and artistic influences were seen everywhere. English gardening magazines had frequent articles about the new Japanese plants, but it was the diplomats and tourist travellers of the 1880s and 1890s who triggered the interest in putting Japanese plants in their proper context – a Japanese garden.

18

Ukiyo-e woodblock print of women in a garden by a stream, filling a *sake* kettle; by Suzuki Harunobe, *c*.1769. Prints of this type gave rare insights into Japanese life. They were increasingly to be found in the West from the early nineteenth century.

Spreading the word

The opening of Japanese ports after 1854 gave rich, curious and intrepid Europeans and Americans a chance to travel. They returned home with stories, photographs and souvenirs of art styles and a culture that was startlingly different from anything that had been seen before. It was a highly refined style, with a definition that had been honed over 250 years of total isolation from any outside influence. The demand to see Japanese art and artefacts was huge. Art shows were mounted in European capitals and in America, and the exhibitions that were so popular in the latter part of the nineteenth century all included some Japanese exhibit.

The Universal Exhibition in London in 1862 included a display of Japanese objects collected by English residents in Yokohama, including examples of *ukiyo-e* (woodblock prints of 'images of the floating world'). The trend continued at the Exposition Universelle in Paris in 1867, where a hundred prints by Hiroshige and others caused great excitement amongst artists and intellectuals. Claude Monet had his own copy of Hiroshige's *Wisteria Blooms over Water at Kameido* amongst a collection of *ukiyo-e* prints, and the famous bridge over the lily-pond in his garden at Giverny is unquestionably Japanese in style. The Vienna Exposition of 1873 was the first to which Japan sent a well-rounded official exhibit, and in 1876 the Centennial Exposition in Philadelphia included a Japanese bazaar with an attached

The Japan–British Exhibition, which took place at White City, west London, in 1910, featured a series of Japanese gardens. (Above left) The gardens in the course of construction. As they were sited immediately at the entrance to White City, the gradual creation of the gardens was the source of great interest. The gardeners appear to be English. (Above right) View of the Garden of Peace, showing the large tea house. (Left) The Garden of the Floating Islands. This was a large and impressive lake with a number of bridges and islands. These photographs are from the *Gardener's Chronicle* of 1910.

garden. The garden has since been developed into the Pine Breeze Villa and Garden in Fairmount Park. In 1903 the Louisiana Purchase Exposition also had an exhibit from Japan – from the Imperial Palace Garden.

In 1910 the Japan–British Exhibition opened in London, one of a series of shows from various nations held at the White City ground near Shepherd's Bush to promote better relations in trade and commerce. The exhibition had been trumpeted for many months in the gardening magazines since it was to include two large – over 10,000 square yards (9000 square metres) – Japanese gardens. In the event it opened very quietly, on 14th May, eight days after the death of Edward VII. The gardens were an instant fascination. One was called the Garden of Peace and included a tea house set beside a lagoon crossed by a number of wooden bridges. The guide book makes no attempt to describe the garden but does state:

> Those who have been in the Far East and have felt, perhaps without understanding, the wonderful significance of such a scene, may well imagine themselves carried away over wide oceans and resting once more in the heart of Romantic Japan.

Information about the second garden is similarly obscure. Called the Garden of the Floating Islands, it was situated near the pavilions of the three newspapers which supported the

Each month *The Garden* magazine published fine illustrations of new and interesting plants.
(Far left) 'The large white Japanese quince', published in 1878.
(Left) 'Two new Japanese camellias', published in 1889.

exhibition, and adjoined a tea house where 'fair maidens of Nippon serve tea and dainties to delighted visitors'. The Japanese Department of Education was careful to say:

> The gardens are not purely Japanese. They manifest the good feeling existing between the horticulturalists of England and Japan; equally they symbolise the alliance between our countries, for Japan supplied the ideas and the plants while Great Britain contributed the site and materials.

By 1910 when the exhibition opened, six gardening journals were published on a monthly or weekly basis in Britain. They had been enthusiastic in their coverage of the introduction of Japanese plants and gardens and now reported at length on the preparation of the garden sites and the landscapes created. There were articles on the plantings of azaleas, aucuba, bamboo, maples and other trees, including mature conifers, all of which were shipped from Japan, as were very large wisterias grown on pergolas. The Japanese had already perfected the transportation of mature trees and shrubs.

In addition to the two large gardens were

Two photographs taken by F. T. Piggott for his book *The Garden of Japan*, an acute observation published in 1896 after he had spent some time living in Japan. (Far left) A dwarf tree of *Prunus mume*. (Left) 'Gardeners going to a flower market with their dwarf trees.' Over one hundred years later gardeners still wear much the same type of clothes.

21

The main gate from the entrance to the Japan–British Exhibition, rebuilt near the Chinese pagoda in the Royal Botanic Gardens at Kew.

two much smaller displays, each on trays about 12 feet by 7 feet (3.7 metres by 2.1 metres). They featured a lake with pine-clad islands, and a rocky promontory with a tea house at the foot of a mountain. These were a novelty to the British public and were much talked of. They represented a quite specific and well-established style of miniature gardening in Japan called *bonkei*. Another garden art form well established in Japan was *bonsai*, which originated in China but had been refined during Japan's years of isolation. It seems to have first caught the attention of the English in the late 1890s, when it was described as 'the dwarfed trees of Japan'. The Yokohama Nursery Company Ltd displayed a collection at White City, together with over two thousand plants and a collection of stone lanterns.

Dozens of Japanese gardeners were shipped to England to create the gardens, bringing plants, ornaments and buildings with them. The ornaments and buildings were almost certainly dispersed afterwards – presumably to the eager creators of new gardens stimulated by what they had seen. Certainly a summer house was removed to the grounds of Bagshot Park in Surrey, then owned by the Duke of Connaught, one of Queen Victoria's sons. It was demolished in 1949, being in 'poor condition'. (One of the first wisteria seedlings to be planted in England was planted at Bagshot Park in 1888.) The main gateway to the exhibition also survived and was eventually rebuilt

View of the Japanese garden at Tatton Park, Cheshire, under construction in 1910. Photographs such as these rarely survive and are vital when restoration work is undertaken.

The Japanese garden at Tatton Park some ninety years after its creation, before a major restoration project was carried out in 2000. Japanese gardens often look at their best in winter sunlight. A light dusting of snow accentuates the angles and shapes of the rocks, ornaments, plants and grasses.

(and restored several times) at the far end of the Royal Botanic Gardens at Kew, where new Japanese gardens were built to complement the gate in 1996.

A number of Japanese gardens were developed soon after the Japan–British Exhibition and records indicate that most of these used Japanese labour (Tully House in County Kildare, Ireland, and Tatton Park in Cheshire for example). It is possible that gardeners stayed on after the exhibition to work on these new gardens. They must have found everything immensely foreign and difficult, from the food and the clothes to the furnishings of the houses. The gardens at Tully House and Tatton Park have both survived, although each has yielded to a Western temptation to let trees and shrubs grow naturally. The creation of the garden at Tatton was, remarkably, photographed for its owner, Alan de Tatton, who had been inspired by a visit to the Japan–British Exhibition. The images are a rare survival showing the original layout and plantings.

The Japanese garden in the West

Diplomats and early travellers were the first to return from Japan inspired to recreate a Japanese garden at home. They were not always entirely comfortable with the methods, but they much admired the general effect and were keen to incorporate new plants into their existing gardens. Algernon Bertram Freeman Mitford, later Lord Redesdale, worked in Japan from 1866 for four years, returning to England to inherit his cousin's estate at Batsford in Gloucestershire. He wrote extensively on bamboos, much admired the trees he saw, but disliked the gardens: 'all spick and span – intensely artificial and a monument to wasted labour'. Reginald Farrer, also a respected plant collector and writer, living in Tokyo in 1903, commented that he thought the Japanese hated plants because they 'butchered' them (he was referring to the severe pruning given to most trees and shrubs). Successful businessmen such as Jeremiah Coleman (Gatton Park in Surrey), Leopold de Rothschild (Gunnersbury Park in West London) and Lord Leverhulme (Rivington in Lancashire) were keen to demonstrate their eye for fashion and knowledge of horticulture by including a Japanese garden in their grounds. Others, such as Lionel de Rothschild, were more interested in the plants. Lionel de Rothschild had contacts with Japanese business for many years and in the 1920s began to

Bamboo pruned in this way can be used in a very small garden to great effect.

(Right) *Rhododendron yakushimanum*, one of two original bushes brought from Japan to Exbury Gardens in Hampshire for the de Rothschild family in the 1920s, at a time when four hundred gardeners worked in the grounds. Countless hybrids have been grown from this stock.

(Below) A glorious sweep of Kurume azaleas at Exbury. Ernest 'Chinese' Wilson first saw these densely flowering azaleas in the town of Kurume in Japan in 1918 and was stunned by the different colours. He sent over two thousand herbarium specimens back from Japan, including many azaleas.

(Below) Conder's illustrations of garden lanterns. Almost obligatory in a Japanese garden, the lantern is a purely Japanese invention with no counterpart in China. Nowadays they rarely contain any kind of illumination.

(Below) Josiah Conder's 'Flat Garden – Rough Style' with minimal planting and carefully trained pine trees; from *Landscape Gardening in Japan*, published in 1893.

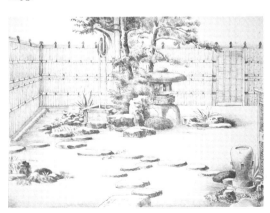

Stone garden bridges illustrated by Conder and much copied in Western gardens.

Light Stone Bridge.

Rustic Slab Bridge.

Stone Trestle Bridge.

Granite Slab Bridge.

Chinese "Full-moon" Bridge.

build his famed collection of rhododendrons and azaleas at Exbury in Hampshire, but he never planned a Japanese garden.

The most influential writer on Japanese gardens was undoubtedly Josiah Conder, who first went to Japan in 1876, having previously worked for the great Victorian architect William Burges. Conder was so smitten by Japan that he emigrated (a very unusual step at that time) and married a Japanese woman. He became an influential architect, working for the Imperial Japanese government. In 1893 his book *Landscape Gardening in Japan* was published in England and swiftly became the seminal work on garden design. In two volumes, copiously illustrated, it covers in detail the ethos of the various types of garden. It includes sketches of various types of garden ornament and photographs of gardens in Japan.

One of the best examples of the newly fashionable Japanese garden was that created in the grounds of Friar Park, near Henley-on-Thames in Oxfordshire, for the rich and eccentric Sir

(Left) Wisteria and a large stone lantern set in a picturesque landscape in Sir Frank Crisp's garden at Friar Park, Henley-on-Thames, Oxfordshire. The photograph was taken in 1906.

(Right) The 'Hill Garden – Finished Style', illustrated by Conder. This influenced Sir Frank Crisp in his designs at Friar Park.

The garden at Hinchingbrooke, Huntingdon, Cambridgeshire, where the Earl of Sandwich installed ornaments and a thatched tea house brought back from Japan. An excellent example of an Edwardian Japanese garden.

Frank Crisp. Crisp had already built himself a miniature Matterhorn and rocky landscape, complete with real chamois, to display his vast collections of alpine plants. The Japanese garden was added in about 1906 and is described at length in the detailed guide book available to the paying public at the time.

Friar Park was constructed following the rules for a 'Hill Garden – Finished Style' in Conder's book, as was the small and private garden at Cottered in Hertfordshire. Cottered was an example of an entire garden turned over to the Japanese style, complete with a miniature Mount Fuji. However, most of the 'Japanese' gardens constructed at the beginning of the twentieth century formed just a part of a much larger garden area. At Hinchingbrooke, near Huntingdon in Cambridgeshire, the Earl of Sandwich, returning from the Far East in 1906, wanted to recreate the 'little landscape of Japan'. In some cases owners wanted to create 'gardens of the world', such as at Fanhams Hall in Hertfordshire, which has also an Austrian house and landscape created in 1900. Japanese gardeners came to Fanhams every

Lilies growing at Coombe Wood, Kingston-upon-Thames, Surrey. Although in private hands, this garden is regularly open under the National Gardens Scheme.

27

The *torii* arch at Compton Acres, Poole, Dorset, unusually flamboyant and leading, not to a Shinto shrine, but to the boundaries of the garden.

summer until the Second World War in order to tend the garden, which had a lake shaped like a fox's head, an authentic Japanese villa, a large number of maples and a replica scaled-down Mount Fuji from which to view the whole. The gardens of Compton Acres in Poole, Dorset, were also created with something of a global theme, with an Italianate garden, a palm court, heather garden and rock and water garden, as well as a Japanese garden. This included a pavilion, summer house, lanterns, a *torii* arch (the usual entrance to a Shinto shrine) and a waterfall tumbling into a large pool with sets of stepping stones. The whole cost the owner, T. W. Simpson, some £220,000 in 1914 (equivalent to about £3 million in 2000).

Perhaps the most interesting of the Japanese gardens built around pools is the earliest, created out of the nurseries laid out by James Herbert Veitch, son of John Gould Veitch, in the 1860s at Coombe Wood in Kingston, Surrey. Row upon row of lilies were grown at Coombe Wood, as well as

The main pool at Compton Acres. The planting is now liberally supported by non-Japanese plants, but the effect is charming. Another example of an early-twentieth-century interpretation of the Japanese style.

Coombe Wood, Surrey: the Japanese gateway entrance to the water gardens framed by overgrown maples and rhododendrons which suit the Western eye.

the trees and shrubs which the Veitch family and their workers brought back from Japan. The water channels and the boggy areas were developed into pools and cascades after the Veitch family sold the area to the owner of neighbouring Warren House. By the 1880s the gardens had already become acclaimed for their Japanese style, although it is quite clear that this was very much in the Victorian idiom, with bright orange pavilions and bridges, trees and shrubs that had long since lost their controlled pruning and irresistible colourful underplanting. The gardens are still maintained as part of the communal gardens for new residential apartments.

Orange or red pavilions and bridges became essential for a 'Japanese' theme in a garden, even though painted pavilions are never seen in Japan, and the red lacquered arched bridge is of Chinese origin. However, at the famous shrines at Nikko, north of Tokyo, the sacred Shinkyo bridge is painted red and often appears in early views of Japan.

(Above) A view inside the water gardens at Coombe Wood, showing mature trees and shrubs no longer pruned to maintain the design of the garden.

(Left) The orange and yellow pavilion at Coombe Wood, incongruous in a Japanese landscape but very much part of the Edwardian interpretation.

(Above left) The red lacquer bridge and thatched pavilion straddling the water-meadow streams at Heale House, Wiltshire. Surrounded by weeping willows and other Western trees, this is a wonderfully picturesque distillation of East and West.

(Above right) The massive stone lantern, standing well over 7 feet (2.1 metres) tall, brought back from Japan by Louis Greville, together with the bridge and pavilion installed at Heale House. In the background are plantings of the gigantic *Gunnera manicata*, from South America, but often found in a Western Japanese garden.

This could explain the presence of the red bridge in Western Japanese gardens. Louis Greville, a diplomat in Tokyo, brought back a bridge and small thatched summer house in 1901. The architect Harold Peto helped design a Japanese area for him at his gardens at Heale House near Salisbury in Wiltshire. Remarkably, both the bridge and the more fragile summer house have survived, as has an impressive stone lantern, and an even more impressive *Cercidyphyllum japonicum*

The pavilion and pergola overlooking the lake in the grounds of Easton Lodge in Essex, photographed c.1920. Designed by Harold Peto in c.1904, the garden is not Japanese but clearly has Japanese overtones with the pavilion architecture, the lantern in the background and the unusual Japanese figures.

The Yokohama Nursery Company's 1906 catalogue, aimed specifically at British and American buyers.

which must have been planted at about the same time, but there is nothing else to suggest the Japanese element. Peto liked to include Japanese-style ornaments in his garden designs; he favoured cranes, which feature at Heale and at Iford, also in Wiltshire, but he never designed a totally Japanese garden. At Easton Lodge in Essex he created a summer house with Japanese overtones and a pergola, presumably for training wisteria, jutting out into a lake, and he added two rather bizarre full-height Japanese figures to set the scene.

As things Japanese became more familiar to the West, garden creators became more selective about the elements they wished to include in their gardens. The new trees, shrubs and flowers were eagerly received. The Yokohama Nursery Company was an active exporter to Britain and to New York from the 1890s, promoting a wide range of plants in its annual catalogues, each with a glorious full-colour cover. It produced special editions for its iris and peony collection and for its lilies, which were immensely popular in England.

In 1906 the nursery claimed it was exporting 5 million bulbs every year – the figure went up to 15 million four years later. Robert Fortune described in detail the way the bulbs were packed, each one individually wrapped in clay for protection during the long months at sea. *Bonsai* were also exported in large numbers, together with a variety of lanterns and containers. Many of the *bonsai* were well over one hundred years old at the time and should still be flourishing one hundred years later. One wonders what has become of the dozens that were sold in Britain.

Before long, English nurseries were offering their own selections of lily bulbs, as well as a vast range of other Japanese-sourced plants, and began calling themselves 'specialist Japanese nurseries'. The nurseries imported

An illustration from the Yokohama Nursery Company's 1905 catalogue.

(Right) Popular images of Japan on catalogue covers from 1925 and 1928 for the Yokohama Nursery Company.

(Below) Illustration from the Yokohama Nursery Company's catalogue of lilies, produced in 1907.

(Above) 'All hands busy sorting *Lilium longiflorum* bulbs', from catalogues of the Yokohama Nursery Company from 1910 and 1914. The Western demand for lilies was huge, although there are several comments in magazines about the sharp practice of some of the Japanese exporters.

(Left) The 1899 Yokohama Nursery Company's catalogue offering 'naninised trees' that had been 'over one hundred years in pots'. Western buyers were fascinated with these miniature trees but probably had little idea how to look after them, despite regular advice in the garden magazines.

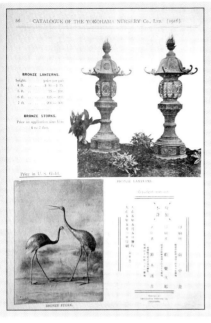

BRONZE LANTERNS.

BRONZE STORKS.

Price in U. S. Gold.

HARDY PLANTS WORTH GROWING.

V. N. GAUNTLETT & Co., Ltd., Japanese Nurseries, Chiddingfold, Surrey.

(Above) V. N. Gauntlett & Company, operating from Chiddingfold in Surrey, was quick to exploit the Japanese theme. This catalogue of *c.*1906 is full of lilies, azaleas, maples and other Japanese shrubs on offer.

(Left) Ornamental lanterns and cranes for export, with prices in dollars. The nursery stipulated terms which included payment in gold if preferred.

their own collections of lanterns and ornaments, selling them on rapidly at a considerable profit. By the 1920s many of the trees and shrubs now so familiar had become part of every nurseryman's normal stock: the azaleas, pines, maples, kerrias, aucubas and skimmias, as well as bulbs and corms, which are now so well represented in Western gardens.

The gardens themselves remained popular during the early decades of the twentieth century, albeit without the huge enthusiasm of earlier years. A few Japanese garden designers

CARTERS JAPANESE LANTERNS

Direct from Japan, made of solid granite, and weighing from 5 cwt. to 1 ton.
Prices from 8 to 25 Guineas. Inspection invited.

Carters of London offered lanterns 'direct from Japan' by the 1920s, 'from 8 to 25 guineas and weighing up to one ton'.

33

Garden Pottery and Ornaments
Impervious to Frost

LIBERTY
REGENT STREET W.1

LIBERTY
REGENT STREET W.1

Liberty of London prided itself on its response to new and exotic markets. Japanese art styles fitted well with its interest in Art Nouveau design. This catalogue dates from c.1910.

(Right) Seyemon Kusumoto is known to have worked on several gardens in south-east England and promoted his work at flower shows.

(Below) Illustration from the catalogue of the Pyghtle showroom in London showing a pergola adapted from a *torii*, one of several garden structures with a Japanese influence.

CHELSEA FLOWER SHOW, 1937

SEYEMON KUSUMOTO, F.R.H.S.
LANDSCAPE ARCHITECT AND CONTRACTOR
8 · MONKVILLE PARADE · TEMPLE FORTUNE · N.W.11.
Also 64, Hendon Way, N.W.2.

established practices in England and Japanese experts continued to advise on garden construction. At Cowden in Perthshire, a famous garden was designed for Ella Christie by a female Japanese designer from Nagoya and was maintained for many years by a Japanese gardener. Out of a boggy, low-lying field, Miss Christie, an intrepid traveller, created her renowned garden in the 1920s, using Korean pines grown from seed, with lilies, azaleas, lanterns and buildings brought from Japan.

Unfortunately the difficulties of creating and, more importantly, maintaining these

The garden at Cowden in Perthshire in the 1950s. Ella Christie, who created the garden, travelled throughout the world, but it was the Japanese landscape which caught her heart and was her great project on her return to Scotland in the 1920s. The garden was vandalised by youths in the 1960s, with the pavilions and bridges damaged and ornaments destroyed.

gardens true to the original have often proved to be overwhelming. Cowden was vandalised by youths in the 1960s and little is left of a once famous garden, save for a few mature pines and shrubs. Of about sixty celebrated Japanese gardens created before the 1950s some have grown wild and been neglected and

Cowden Japanese garden was designed and overseen by Taki Honda, a woman designer from Nagoya. It was maintained for over ten years from 1925 by Matsuo, a Japanese gardener who never learnt to speak much English and is buried in the local churchyard.

A Japanese wood and paper house, seen behind the fall of pale pink cherry blossom. A typical Japanese view, it is part of a garden in southern England, created in 1905 and restored by Seyemon Kusomoto in 1923. It is one of the few gardens to survive almost intact over the years and is still private property.

many others have all but disappeared. As houses have changed hands the history of the gardens has been forgotten and very little early photographic evidence has survived. But, as interest in Oriental culture is revived at the beginning of the twenty-first century, many of the gardens, such as Tatton, Gunnersbury and Rivington, are being rediscovered and restored; others are being created, such as at Holland Park, London, near the site of an earlier garden. There is a renewed fascination with the aesthetic of the Japanese garden.

In 1915 Laurence Weaver, editor of *Country Life*, wrote: 'The disposition of a few typical ornaments, of a bronze stork here and a stone lantern there, does not make a Japanese garden; it only makes an English garden speak with a Japanese voice.' Gardens in the United Kingdom have

A large snow-viewing lantern or *yukimi-gata* (so called because of the way the snow is held on the roof), placed in a traditional position beside water, with clipped 'cloud' pines behind. It is part of a remarkable Japanese garden still in private hands, first created in 1905. This is a surprising Japanese scene in the heart of south-east England, complete with lakes, lanterns, buildings and bridges.

A new Japanese house and garden built in central London, c.2000, designed by Takashi Sawano. It is hugely expensive to maintain such a garden's correct appearance, an aspect of Japanese garden projects that is often over-looked.

tended not to follow strictly the principles of Japanese garden design, for example the concern for borrowed scenery, or the vital balances in the asymmetry. However, the temptation in English gardens to let trees and shrubs grow naturally, and particularly to allow colour to take over, has in many cases evolved into a very successful hybrid of Japanese and western elements.

(Right) A *karesansui* garden designed by Takashi Sawano c.2000 captures the timeless and soothing effect of the earlier raked gravel gardens. The garden is deliberately designed to comp-lement the views from the large windows of the house.

The new garden at Holland Park in London was built in 1991 as part of the Japan Festival that year. An earlier garden, built in the early part of the twentieth cen-tury close to this spot, has now disappeared with the exception of an overgrown clump of bamboo and a few mature pine trees.

Further reading

Bibb, Elizabeth. *In the Japanese Garden.* Starwood Publishing, 1991.

Cave, Philip. *Creating Japanese Gardens.* Aurum Press, 1993.

Curtis' Botanical Magazine, volume 16, part 2. Royal Horticultural Society, May 1999. (Specialist issue on the introduction of Japanese plants to the West.)

Earle, Joe (editor). *Infinite Spaces.* Galileo, 2000. (Photographs and words based on the *Sakuteiki*.)

Glattstein, Judy. *Enhance Your Garden with Japanese Plants.* Kodansha International, 1996. (Available in the UK.)

Itoh, Teiji. *The Gardens of Japan.* Kodansha International, 1998. (Available in the UK.)

King, Ronald. *The Quest for Paradise.* Whittet Books, 1979.

Oster, Maggie. *Japanese Garden Style.* Cassell, 1993.

Sawano, Takashi. *Creating Your Own Japanese Garden.* Shufunotomo, 1999. (Available in the UK.)

The following earlier books can be read at the Lindley Library at the Royal Horticultural Society, 80 Vincent Square, London SW1P 2PE.

Conder, Josiah. *Landscape Gardening in Japan.* 1893.

Conder, Josiah. *Supplement to Landscape Gardening in Japan.* 1893.

Du Cane, Florence. *The Flowers and Gardens of Japan.* 1906.

Veitch, James Herbert. *Hortus Veitchii.* 1906.

A hill garden at Shoen-in temple in Kyoto. 'When the Buddha preached he stood under a tree. When the Shinto gods come down from heaven they take up residence in trees. So is it not essential that human habitations should be surrounded by trees?' (from the eleventh-century *Sakuteiki*, or *Essay on Garden-making*.)

Places to visit

Batsford Arboretum, Batsford Park, Moreton-in-Marsh, Gloucestershire GL56 9QB. Telephone: 01386 701441. Begun as a collection of trees, particularly maples and bamboos brought back from Japan by Bertram Mitford, later Lord Redesdale, after his time there in the 1860s. He also brought back lanterns and ornaments but did not create a Japanese garden.

Capel Manor Gardens, Bullsmoor Lane, Enfield, Middlesex EN1 4RQ. Telephone: 020 8366 4442. Now a horticultural college. The grounds, which have gardens on many themes, include a Japanese-style garden.

Compton Acres, 164 Canford Cliffs Road, Poole, Dorset BH13 7ES. Telephone: 01202 700778. Website: www.comptonacres.co.uk A series of 'gardens of the world', including an early Japanese example.

Exbury Gardens, Exbury, Southampton, Hampshire SO45 1AZ. Telephone: 023 8089 1203. The gardens have never included a Japanese garden but have famous displays of azaleas, including many of the Japanese varieties.

Gatton Park, Reigate, Surrey. The subject of a television series following the restoration of historic gardens, this Japanese garden was originally created by the Coleman family in the first decade of the twentieth century.

Gunnersbury Park, London W3 8LQ. Telephone: 020 8992 1612. Garden built in the grounds of his mansion by Leopold de Rothschild in 1906. Plans for complete renovation developed in 2001.

Heale House, Woodford, Salisbury, Wiltshire SP4 6NT. Telephone: 01722 782504. Bridge and summer house incorporated into water meadows.

Holland Park, Kensington, London. A garden to commemorate the Japan Festival of 1991 was opened near the site of a garden that was built in the 1930s but which has now almost disappeared.

Irish National Stud and Japanese Gardens, Tully, Kildare, County Kildare, Eire. Telephone: 00353 45 521617. Website: www.irish-national-stud.ie A renowned Japanese garden built c.1906, now with other gardens and the National Stud.

Newstead Abbey Park, Ravenshead, Nottinghamshire NG15 8GE. Telephone: 01623 455900. Website: www.newsteadabbey.org.uk A 'Japanese' garden was built in the grounds of Lord Byron's former home in 1910.

Parasampra, Donnington Grove Country Club, Donnington, Newbury, Berkshire RG14 2LA. Telephone: 01635 552217. Open only by appointment. A Japanese garden was originally built in the grounds in the early years of the twentieth century.

Rivington, Lancashire. Japanese water gardens were created by Lord Leverhulme from 1902 onwards and opened in 1919. Now owned by the North-West Water Authority, the grounds are being restored.

Royal Botanic Gardens, Kew, Richmond, Surrey TW9 3AB. Telephone: 020 8332 5000. Website: www.rbgkew.org.uk The gate from the Japan–British Exhibition was removed to Kew and rebuilt near the Chinese pagoda. It was restored in November 1995 and is now complemented by a Japanese garden completed in October 1996.

Savill Garden, Wick Lane, Englefield Green, Surrey TW20 0UU. Telephone: 01753 847518. Website: www.savillgarden.co.uk Not strictly a Japanese garden, but celebrated collections of azaleas and other shrubs from Japan.

Tatton Park, Knutsford, Cheshire WA16 6QN. Telephone: 01625 534400. Japanese garden constructed in 1910 for Alan de Tatton. Includes tea house and small shrine. Completely restored in 2001.

The lists of gardens that are part of the National Gardens Scheme and the National Gardens Scheme of Scotland should be consulted, as some gardens are in private hands but are occasionally open to the public. Others, such as the Water Gardens (Coombe Wood) and Fanhams Hall, are now private institutions but do open their gardens, usually through the Scheme.

The Japan Society, Morley House, 6th Floor, 314–322 Regent Street, London W1B 3BQ.
Telephone: 020 7636 3029. Website: www.japansociety.org.uk
The Japan Society has an educational objective, providing lectures and publications, together with visits and other events, to further the mutual understanding of the cultures of Britain and Japan. It has a full programme of events and further information on related topics.

Japanese gardens in the United States
Atlanta Botanical Garden, Atlanta, Georgia; Bellingrath Gardens, Theodore, Alabama; Brooklyn Botanic Garden; Chicago Botanic Garden, Glencoe, Illinois; Dawes Arboretum, Newark, Ohio; Fairmount Park, Philadelphia, Pennsylvania; Golden Gate Park, California; Japanese Garden, Portland, Oregon; John P. Humes Stroll Garden, Mill Neck, New York; Missouri Botanical Garden, St Louis, Missouri.

Ukiyo-e woodblock print, 'Wisteria blooms over water at Kameido', from *One Hundred Views of Edo* by Hiroshige (1797–1858). The French artist Monet is known to have had a copy of this print. Such prints were rare illustrations of Japan in the West.